LIVING IN GOSHEN

Let My People Go!

Elijah Centre
Project
Heritage

Let My People Go!

Based on the "Living in Goshen" Series
Created by Elijah Centre Project Heritage

© 2020 Congress Publishing House
All rights reserved.

Originally printed in Trinidad & Tobago
First Printing 2020

ISBN 978-976-43-0021-2

Congress
Publishing **House**

Dedicated to the Children of Congress WBN

Keep Goshen in your hearts!

For 400 years
We lived under strain.

4

Harsh Pharaoh was grim,

We endured the pain.

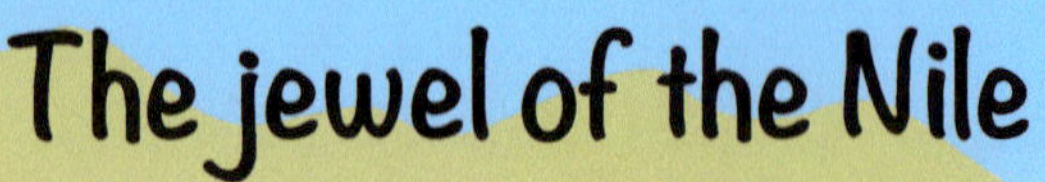

The jewel of the Nile

Was

Egypt

so fair.

Such riches and glory!
Such pomp and
such flair!

Then Moses was raised up
With his brother, Aaron, too.

God spoke to them both:
"YOU'VE GOT SOME WORK TO DO!"

With his rod in his hand, Aaron
at his side,
Moses then declared, in humility,
not pride...

"LET MY PEOPLE GO!"

"I will not let
them go."

"LET MY PEOPLE GO!"

"My power I
will show!"

In Egypt... the plagues began.
Our God, He had a plan!

1

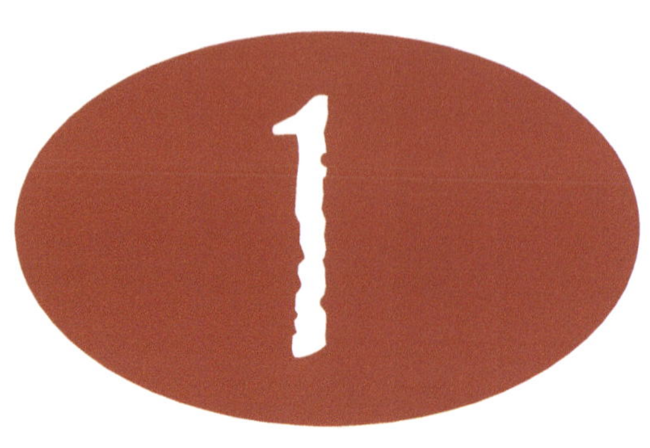

One...

the Nile turned ruby red.

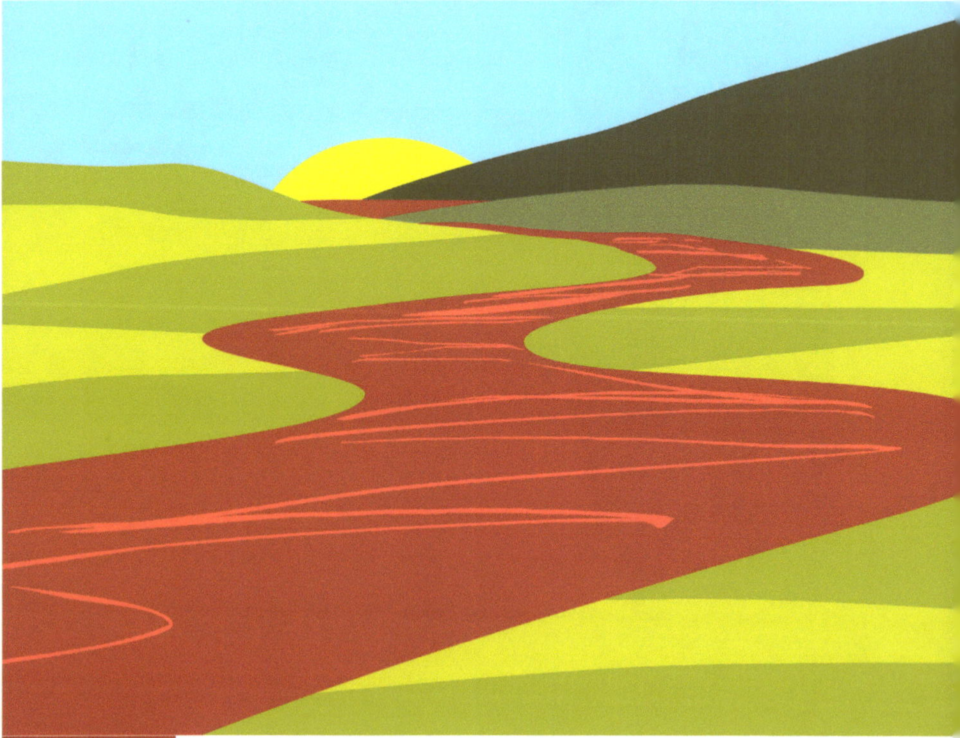

Two...

the frogs were everywhere:
Frogs below, frogs on high,
In their beds making them cry!

3

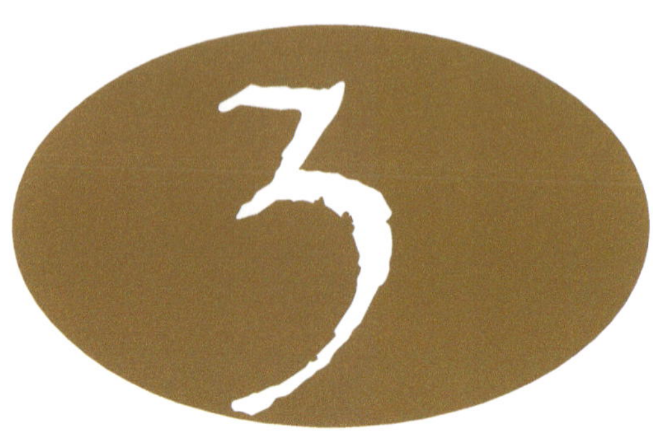

Three...

there were the sickening lice.

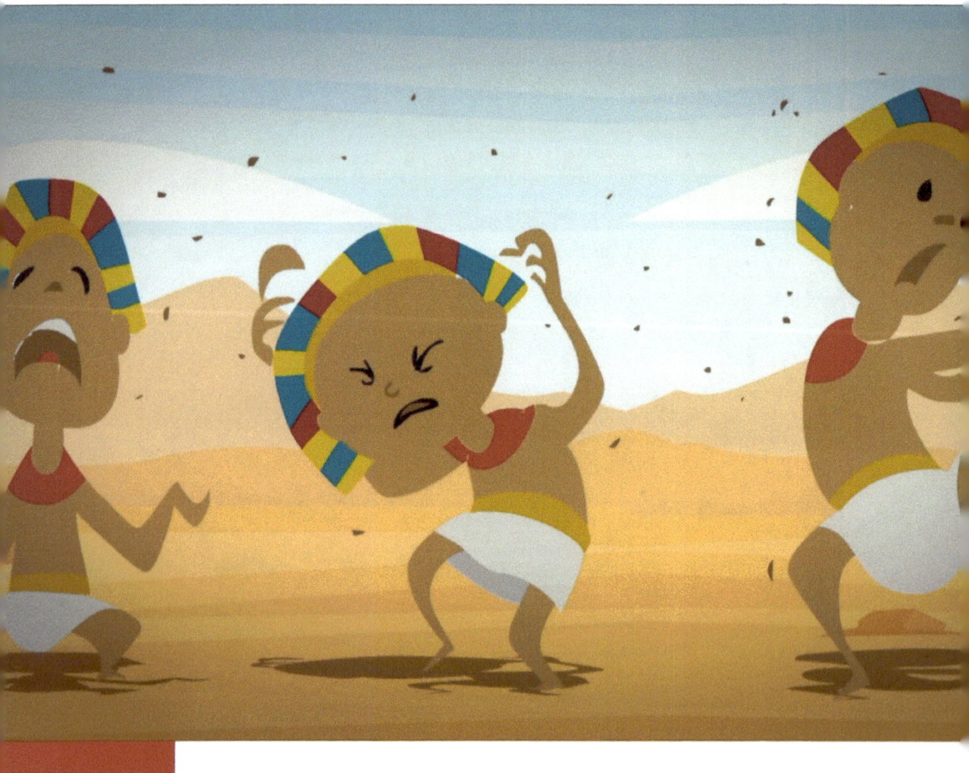

4

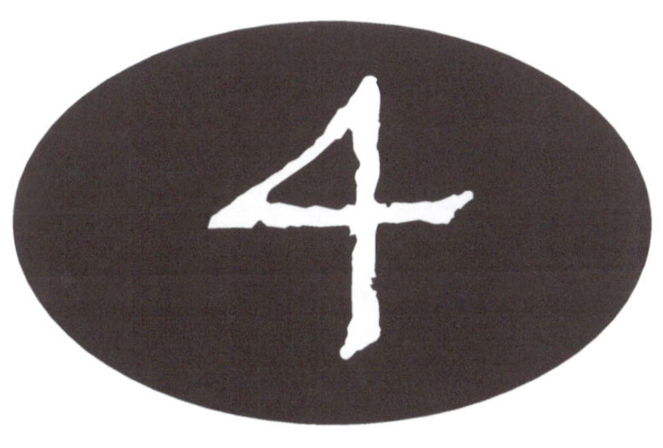

Four...

flies of every size.

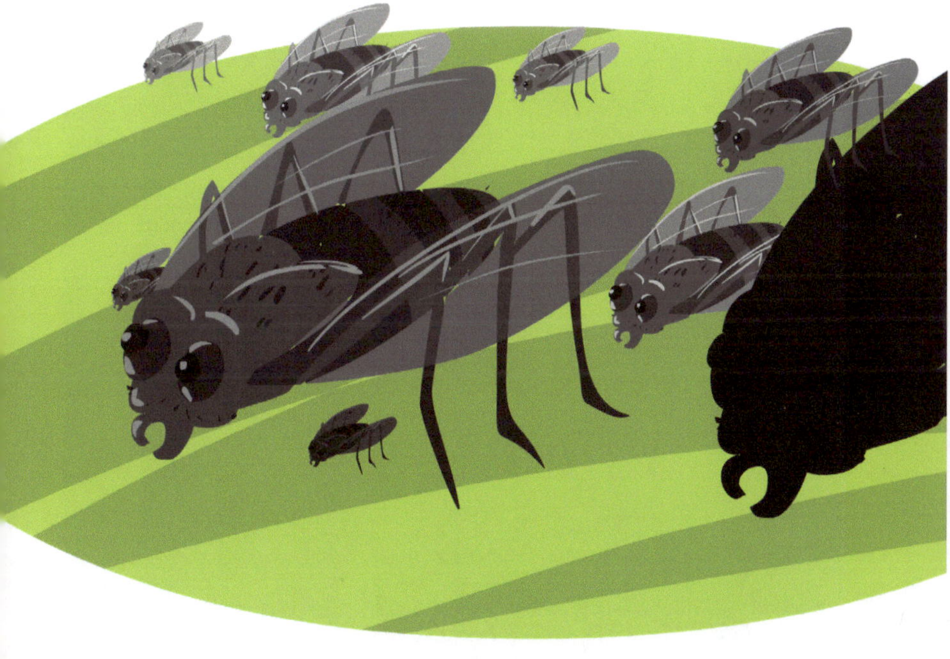

Five...

the death of all livestock too...
What were the Egyptians to do?

"I will not let them go."

Six...

Oh my, the nasty boils.

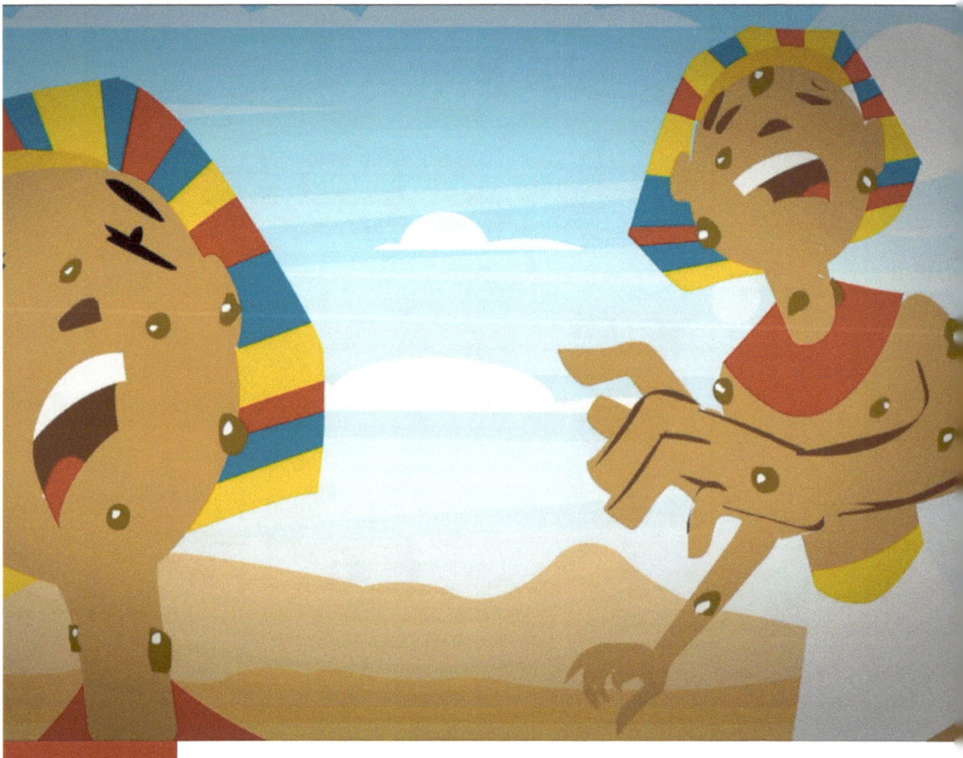

Seven...

Ice fell out from the skies.

8

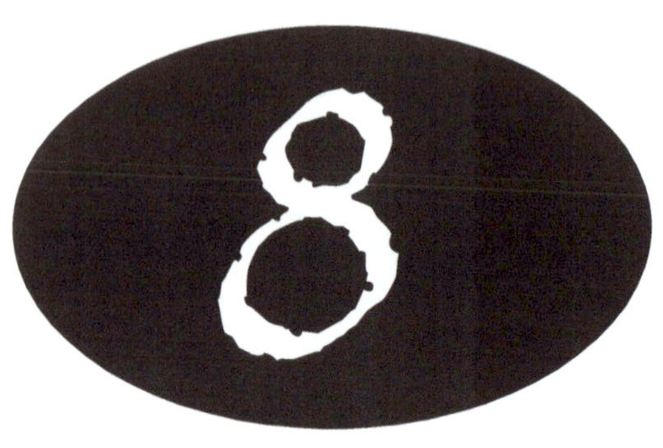

Eight...
locusts flew all in.

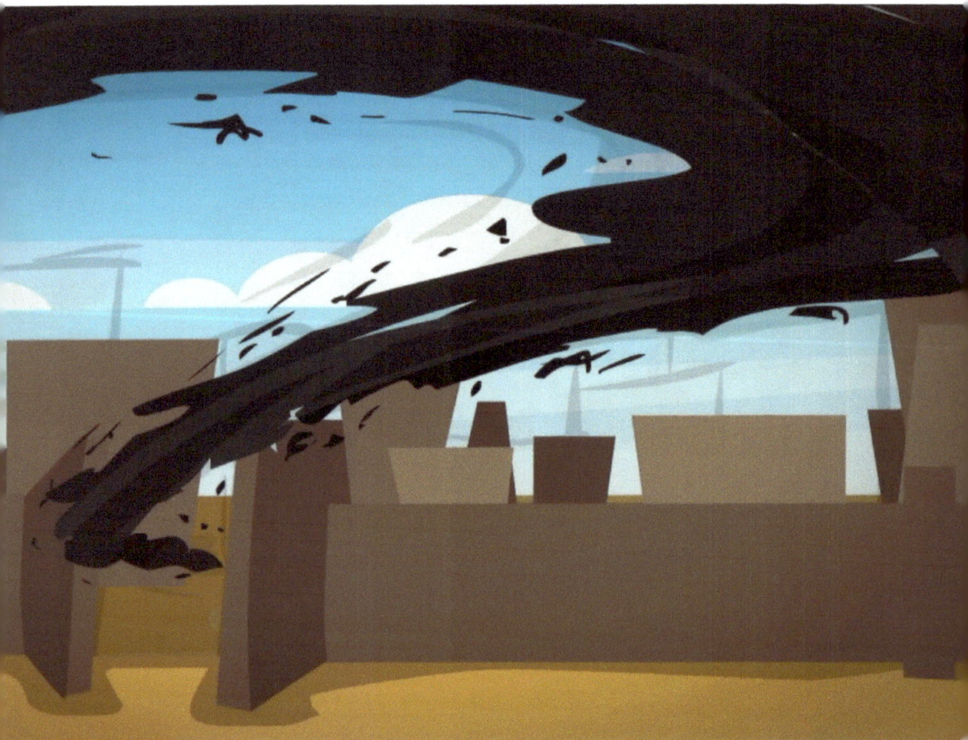

Nine...
darkness black as sin.

And **Ten**...
the worst on the list...

The firstborn all gone and
all missed!!!

"...Oh fine, I'll let you go."

"Thank God, you let us go!"

Make haste,
don't move too slow.

We've got to go!

Riders stomped in haste.

They had no time to waste!

Before us the crimson tide,

Nowhere to run or hide!

"I will not let you go."

"YOU HAVE TO LET US GO!"

"I will not let you go."

"LET US GO!"

Jehovah our help and aid,
Your love will never fade!

Remove this horrid foe,
He simply has to go!!!

We followed our leader
Through the Red Sea we trod.

Protection, like in Goshen

Our God had kept His word!

But for Pharaoh, that loser,
What was his doom?
His army under waters
To a sudden gloom.

"I will not let you go."
"LET US GO!"

TH...
HO...
AND
RI...

THROWN

THE S...

Our God has come and given the

victory.

Oh! The foe is gone.
He's no longer here!
Our God has come,
There's nothing to fear!!!

I...

had...

to...

let them go...

GOD MADE HIM
LET US GO!

"Living in Goshen" was produced by Elijah Centre Project Heritage.

Elijah Centre is a unique, global, borderless, Kingdom community, founded on biblical principles and recognizing Jesus Christ as its head. With its primary base in Trinidad & Tobago, called the Nexus, Elijah Centre has locations in cities around the globe, referred to as Embassies. For more information, visit:

www.elijahcentre.org

Project Heritage is the People Group ministry within Elijah Centre for children up to age 11. Project Heritage focuses on holistic development based on the pattern of maturity demonstrated by Jesus throughout his childhood. For more information, visit:

www.projectheritage.org

Elijah Centre is the Creative Core of Congress WBN, a global, faith-based organization affecting human, social and national transformation throughout the earth. For more information, visit:

www.congresswbn.org